JUST LIKE A HERO

WRITTEN & ILLUSTRATED BY
VLADIMIR SAINTE

Contact the author at vladimirsainte@gmail.com

ISBN-13:978-1-942005-44-5

Content X Design, Inc.
PO Box 8754, Kansas City, MO 64114

I would first like to thank Bryan Nigh for helping make my dream a reality; to take my hand-drawn illustrations and make them digital was beyond my expertise. Next I would like to thank Lena Anderson for being my editor/wordsmith and catching all my grammatical errors.

To my children, Oden and Alivia, daddy loves you very much.

Last, but most importantly, I would like to thank my wife, Clara Anderson Sainte, for always seeing my worth and pushing me toward growth and change.

DEAR READERS,

THROUGHOUT MY CAREER AS A THERAPIST, I HAVE
WORKED WITH CHILDREN WHO HAVE STRUGGLED TO
KNOW THEIR WORTH. THEY ARE THE INSPIRATION
BEHIND THIS BOOK. OFTEN CHILDREN NEED A
REMINDER OF HOW IMPORTANT THEY REALLY ARE.
WHEN WE TREAT EACH OTHER (AND OURSELVES) WITH
DIGNITY AND RESPECT, IT HELPS THE WORLD TURN A
LITTLE EASIER. EVERYONE HAS THE POTENTIAL FOR
GREATNESS – IT JUST TAKES A LITTLE LOVE,
NURTURING SUPPORT, AND SEEING YOURSELF AS A
HERO.

Vladimir Sainte

THIS IS WILL.
THERE ARE TIMES WHEN
HE CAN ONLY SEE
NEGATIVE THINGS
ABOUT HIMSELF.

BUT JUST LIKE A *HERO*,
WILL CAN BE *OPEN-MINDED*
AND ACCEPT COMPLIMENTS
FROM PEOPLE
WHO CARE ABOUT HIM.

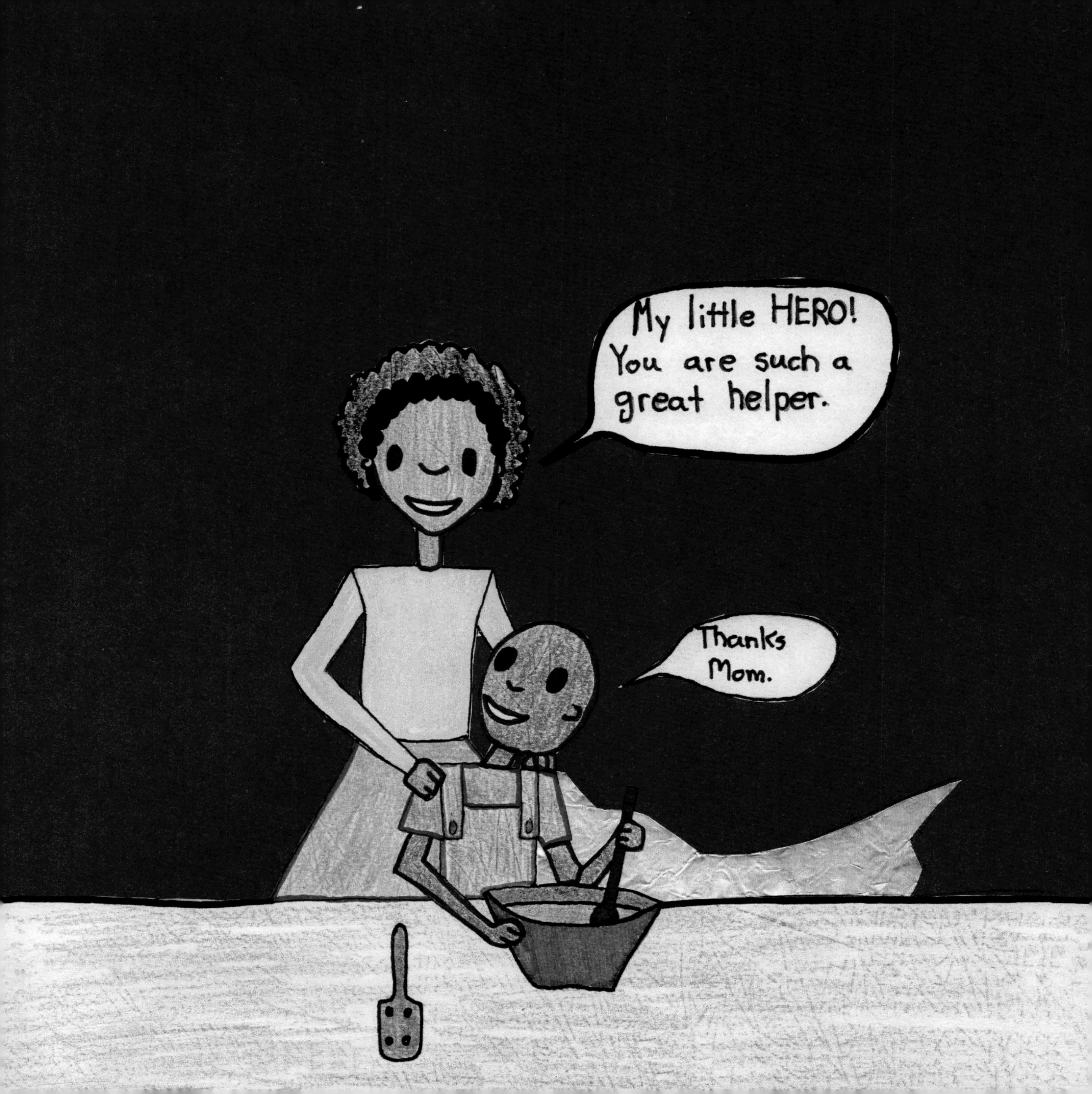
My little HERO! You are such a great helper.
Thanks Mom.

SOMETIMES WILL THINKS
ABOUT THINGS THAT MAKE HIM
FEEL REALLY MAD.

HE SHOWS THIS BIG FEELING BY
BEING MEAN AND ANGRY TO HIS
FRIEND CARRIE.

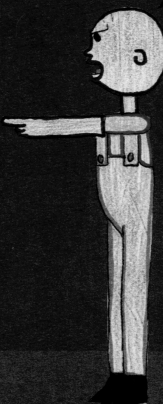

BUT JUST LIKE A *HERO*,
WILL CAN BE *BRAVE*
AND TALK TO AN ADULT HE TRUSTS
ABOUT HIS HURT FEELINGS.

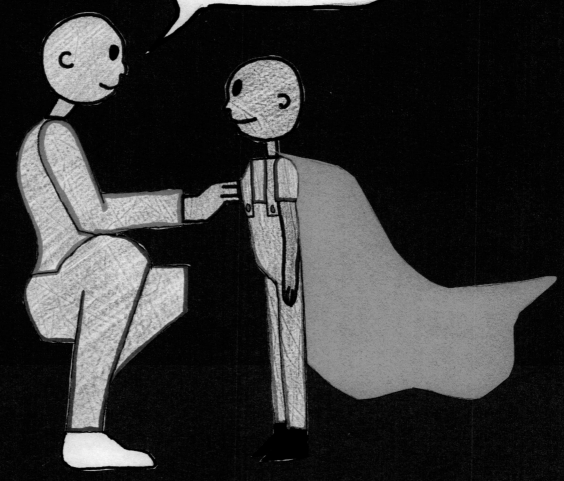

THERE ARE TIMES WHEN
WILL FEELS LIKE
HE JUST CAN'T DO IT.

BUT JUST LIKE A *HERO*,
HE CAN BE *STRONG*
AND ASK A MENTOR
OR TEACHER FOR HELP.

WILL CAN THINK POSITIVELY
BY TELLING HIMSELF,
"YES I CAN."

THERE ARE TIMES
WHEN WILL FINDS
IT HARD TO
THINK BEFORE HE ACTS.

BUT JUST LIKE A *HERO*,
WILL CAN PRACTICE
BEING *PATIENT*
BY TAKING DEEP BREATHS
IN AND OUT BEFORE HE ACTS.

CAN YOU HELP WILL
PUT OUT THE FIRE?

Deep Breath In.....

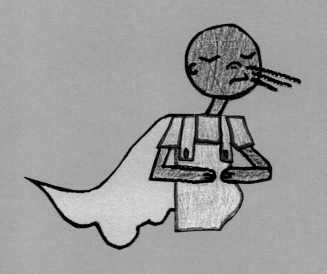

Help Us

Slow Breath Out.....

Thank You

SOMETIMES IT'S HARD
FOR WILL TO ACCEPT
RESPONSIBILITY FOR
HIS BAD CHOICES.

BUT JUST LIKE A *HERO*,
WILL CAN BE *HONEST*
AND LEARN FROM HIS MISTAKES.

SOMETIMES WILL AND
HIS LITTLE SISTER, ROSIE,
JUST DON'T GET ALONG.

BUT JUST LIKE A *HERO*,
HE CAN BE A *HELPFUL*
BIG BROTHER WHEN
ROSIE NEEDS HIM MOST.

WILL NOW UNDERSTANDS
HE CAN USE HIS *SUPERPOWERS*
TO TURN NEGATIVE THOUGHTS INTO
POSITIVE ONES...

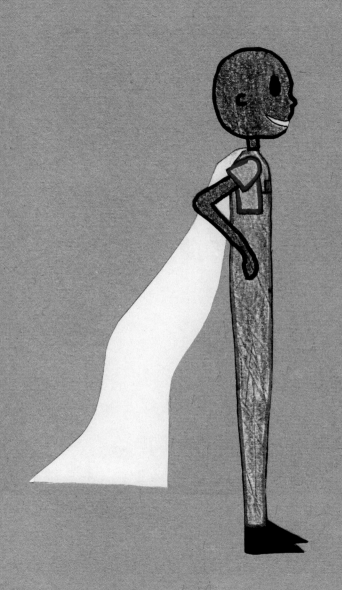

...AND HE'S READY TO
TAKE ON THE WORLD.

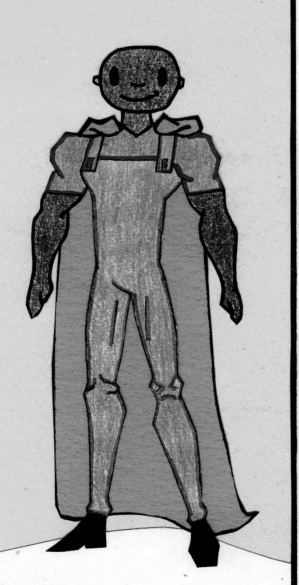

POWERS/SKILLS

BELOW ARE WILL'S SUPERPOWERS. EACH ABILITY INCLUDES HEALTHY ACTIVITIES TO PROMOTE STRONGER SELF-ESTEEM, EFFECTIVE COPING MECHANISMS, AND POSITIVE THINKING. THE PRIMARY GOAL IS TO CREATE A POSITIVE INTERACTION WHILE READING THIS BOOK WITH A CHILD, AND HELP THEM UNDERSTAND THAT CERTAIN BEHAVIORS ARE PART OF NORMAL DEVELOPMENT.

NOTE: CHILDREN ARE NATURALLY RESILIENT, AND WHEN PROPERLY SUPPORTED, THEY CAN COPE WITH NUMEROUS ADVERSITIES/PROBLEMS AND ADJUST TO THEIR ENVIRONMENT.

• *I-FACTOR:* ABILITY TO USE CONFLICT RESOLUTION SKILLS SUCH AS "I MESSAGES" AND ASSERTIVENESS PATTERNS OF COMMUNICATION TO EXPRESS EMOTIONS PROPERLY

• *CONFIDENCE ENHANCER:* ABILITY TO IMPLEMENT AGE-APPROPRIATE COPING SKILLS TO MANAGE BIG FEELINGS (I.E., PHYSICAL EXERCISE, MEDITATION, MANDALA COLORING SHEETS, POSITIVE MANTRA "YES, I CAN", ETC.)

• *ENHANCED CONDITION:* ABILITY TO USE SELF-CONTROL STRATEGIES (I.E., DEEP BREATHING, COUNTING BACKWARDS FROM TEN, ETC.), TO DELAY DESIRE FOR INSTANT GRATIFICATION

• *VIRTUE INDUCEMENT:* ABILITY TO KNOW THE VALUE OF BEING HONEST (I.E., FORGING TRUST WITHIN RELATIONSHIPS), BY CONSTANTLY IDENTIFYING THE BENEFITS OF BEING TRUTHFUL

DRAW YOUR SUPERHERO HERE.

With more than eight years' experience as a therapist, Vladimir Sainte, Licensed Clinical Social Worker, has made an invaluable impact on the Kansas City community through his work as counselor and crisis clinician. Sainte is committed to providing supportive counseling, not just with children, but through a partnership with their families and the broader community members for a holistic impact on the child's development. Sainte graduated with a Bachelor of Arts in Sociology and a Master of Social Work from the University of Missouri-Kansas City.

Follow Sainte on Instagram at **vla1899**

Made in the USA
Columbia, SC
05 March 2019